EASY GENIUS MATH
ALGEBRA AND PRE-ALGEBRA
IT'S EASY!

x^2+y^2

FREE WORKSHEETS AVAILABLE
www.enslow.com

$3x^2y$

$(a^2+b^2)=$

x^2+y^2

$3x^2y$

$\dfrac{1}{2(m+}$

$(a^2+b^2)=c^2$

Rebecca Wingard-Nelson

Enslow Publishers, Inc.
40 Industrial Road
Box 398
Berkeley Heights, NJ 07922
USA

http://www.enslow.com

Original edition published as *Algebra and Pre-Algebra* in 2008.

Library of Congress Cataloging-in-Publication Data

Wingard-Nelson, Rebecca.
    Algebra and pre-algebra : it′s easy/Rebecca Wingard-Nelson.
        pages cm. — (Easy genius math)
    Previously published as: Algebra and pre-algebra. ©2008.
    Summary:"Learn about variables, integers, expressions, and absolute values. Practice
order of operations and multi-step problems"— Provided by publisher.
    Includes bibliographical references.
    ISBN 978-0-7660-4251-3
    1. Algebra—Juvenile literature. 2. Mathematics—Juvenile literature. I. Title.
    QA155.15.W562 2014
    512.9—dc23

                                                   2012042852

Future editions:
Paperback ISBN: 978-1-4644-0445-0
Single-User PDF ISBN: 978-1-4646-1242-8

EPUB ISBN: 978-1-4645-1242-1
Multi-User PDF ISBN: 978-0-7660-5874-3

Printed in the United States of America

102013 Lake Book Manufacturing, Inc., Melrose Park, IL

10 9 8 7 6 5 4 3 2 1

To Our Readers: We have done our best to make sure all Internet addresses in this book were active and appropriate when we went to press. However, the author and the publisher have no control over and assume no liability for the material available on those Internet sites or on other Web sites they may link to. Any comments or suggestions can be sent by e-mail to comments@enslow.com or to the address on the back cover.

♻ Enslow Publishers, Inc., is committed to printing our books on recycled paper. The paper in every book contains 10% to 30% post-consumer waste (PCW). The cover board on the outside of each book contains 100% PCW. Our goal is to do our part to help young people and the environment too!

Illustration Credits: ©Artville/Artzooks, p. 7; Jennet Chua/Photos.com, p. 31; Katerina Stepanova/Photos.com, p. 32; Photos.com, pp. 14, 17, 19, 22, 23, 39, 51; Shutterstock.com, pp. 11, 21, 27, 29, 37, 41, 43, 47, 49, 55, 56; Timothy Carillet/Photos.com, p. 17.

Cover Photo: PIKSEL/Photos.com

CONTENTS

Introduction

Not every person is an accountant, engineer, rocket scientist, or math teacher. However, every person does use math.

Most people never think, "I just used math to decide if I have enough milk for this week!" But that is exactly what they did. Math is everywhere; we just don't see it all the time because it doesn't always look like the math we do at school.

Math gives you the power to:
• determine the best route on a trip
• keep score in a game
• choose the better buy
• figure a sale price
• plan a vacation schedule

How can you describe a value that changes? For example, if you make $8 an hour, your pay changes with the number of hours you work. Algebra is a mathematical way to describe how things change (like your paycheck), and how things are related (like the amount you earn and how long you work).

This book will help you understand algebra and pre-algebra. It can be read from beginning to end, or used to review a specific topic.

① Integers

You can use different types of numbers to show different values.

Types of Numbers

natural, or counting, numbers—The numbers you use to count.

$$1, 2, 3, 4, 5, \ldots$$

whole numbers—The natural numbers and zero.

$$0, 1, 2, 3, 4, 5, \ldots$$

integers—Whole numbers and their opposites.

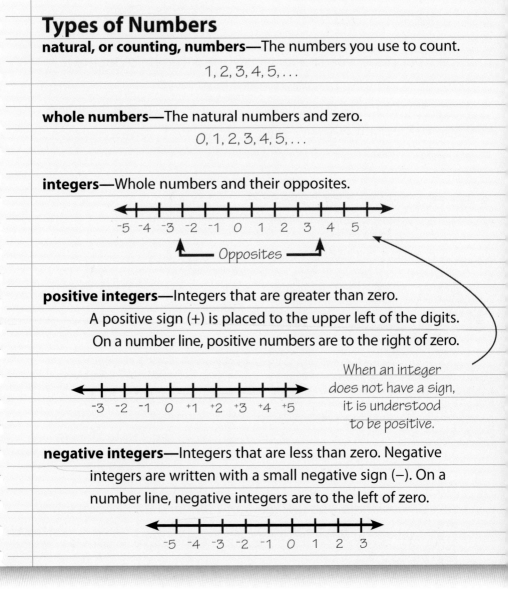

positive integers—Integers that are greater than zero.
A positive sign (+) is placed to the upper left of the digits.
On a number line, positive numbers are to the right of zero.

When an integer does not have a sign, it is understood to be positive.

negative integers—Integers that are less than zero. Negative integers are written with a small negative sign (−). On a number line, negative integers are to the left of zero.

Opposites

What integer is the opposite of ⁺2?

Step 1: Opposite integers are the same distance from zero on a number line, but on opposite sides. The integer ⁺2 is two units to the right of zero. Find the integer that is two units to the left of zero.

-⁴ ⁻3 ⁻2 ⁻1 0 ⁺1 ⁺2 ⁺3 ⁺4

2 1 | 1 2

The opposite of ⁺2 is ⁻2.

Opposite numbers use the same digits but different signs.

+2 is read as "positive two."

–2 is read as "negative two."

Using Integers

What integer can be used to represent a temperature of 40°C below zero?

Step 1: Negative integers are less than zero.
Since the temperature is below zero, use a negative integer.

The integer ⁻40 can represent 40°C below zero.

What integer can be used to show a gain of 7 yards in a football game?

Step 1: Integers can be used to show gain or loss. A gain is represented by a positive integer. A loss is represented by a negative integer.

The integer ⁺7, or 7, can represent a gain of 7 yards.

What integer can be used to show a debt of $5?

Step 1: Integers can be used to show amounts you owe (debt) or amounts you have. Amounts you have are positive. Amounts you owe are negative.

The integer ⁻5 can represent a debt of $5.

② Rationals

Rational numbers are any numbers
that can be written as fractions.

Types of Numbers

rational numbers (rationals)—Numbers that can be written as
a ratio, or fraction. For example, $^2/_3$ is a rational number.
Any integer can be written as a fraction with a
denominator of one ($2 = {^2/_1}$). So, all integers are
rational numbers.

Examples of rational numbers: $^-3$, 0, 1/2, 0.6, 4 2/3, 5

Rational numbers can be positive or negative. Zero is also a
rational number ($0 = {^0/_1}$). Rational numbers have opposites
that are the same distance from zero on a number line.

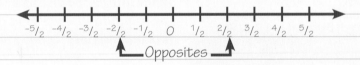

irrational numbers (irrationals)—Numbers that cannot be
written as a ratio. Decimals that do not end and do not
repeat are irrational numbers.

Examples of irrational numbers: π (3.141592653589793...),
$\sqrt{5}$ (2.2360679774997...), $-7.5138244956422397...$

real numbers—The set of all rational and irrational numbers.

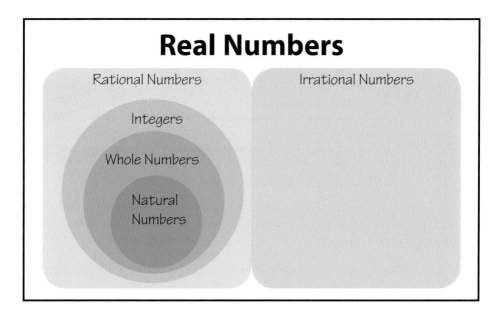

Real Numbers

Rational Numbers

Irrational Numbers

Integers

Whole Numbers

Natural Numbers

Classifying Numbers

Diagrams like the one above show how the sets of numbers are related. You can use a diagram like this to find all of the names that apply to a number.

Tell all the names that apply to the number ⁻3.

Step 1: Look at the diagram. Begin in natural numbers. Is ⁻3 a natural number?

No. Natural numbers are counting numbers.

Step 2: In the diagram, move out one section to whole numbers. Is ⁻3 a whole number?

No. Whole numbers are all positive.

Step 3: Is ⁻3 an integer?

Yes. Integers are the whole numbers and their opposites.

Step 4: Look at the diagram.
The set of integers is inside the set of rational numbers.
The set of rational numbers is inside the set of real numbers.
Since ⁻3 is an integer it is also a rational number, and a real number. Integers are not inside the set of irrational numbers.

−3 is an integer, a rational number and a real number.

9

③ Comparing Numbers

You can use a number line to understand how positive and negative numbers are compared.

Number Lines

All rational numbers can be shown on a number line.
On the number line, numbers are greater as you move right.
Numbers are smaller as you move left.

Ordering Numbers

Put the numbers 2, ⁻4, 0, ⁻1 in order from least to greatest.

Step 1: Look at the numbers on a number line.

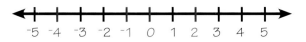

On a number line, numbers are in order from least to greatest. The least, or smallest, number is the farthest left. The greatest number is the farthest right.

Step 2: Write the numbers in order beginning on the left.

From least to greatest, the numbers are:

  −4, −1, 0, 2

Comparison Symbols

The **equal sign (=)** shows that two numbers have the same value.

$$1 = \frac{2}{2}$$

Inequality symbols are used to compare numbers that have different values.

The **less than sign (<)** shows that the first number "is less than" the second.

3 < 7

The **greater than sign (>)** shows that the first number "is greater than" the second.

1 > ⁻5

Comparing Numbers

The temperature Monday was ⁻5°F.
The temperature Tuesday was ⁻3°F.
Compare ⁻5°F and ⁻3°F.
Which day was warmer?

Step 1: Look at the numbers on a number line.

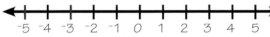

Step 2: Compare the numbers using an inequality symbol.

⁻5 < ⁻3 so, ⁻5°F < ⁻3°F

Step 3: A greater temperature is warmer. Since ⁻5°F < ⁻3°F, the greater temperature is ⁻3°F.

Tuesday was warmer than Monday.

Comparing a positive number and a negative number is easy!

Positive numbers are always greater than negative numbers.

11

④ Absolute Value

Opposite numbers are the same distance from zero on a number line. The distance a number is from zero is important enough to have its own name.

Absolute Value

The **absolute value** of a number is the distance the number is from zero on a number line.

Absolute value is always a positive number.

The symbol for absolute value is vertical lines around a number.

The absolute value of ⁻7 is written as |⁻7|.

Positive Numbers

Find the value of |3|.

Step 1: Find the distance from zero to the number inside the absolute value sign, 3. You can find the distance by counting the number of units from 0 to 3 on a number line.

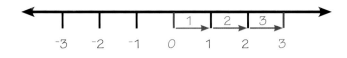

The distance is 3 units.

|3| = 3

> The absolute value of every positive number is the same as the number.
>
> |5| = 5 |0.8| = 0.8 $\left|\frac{1}{2}\right| = \frac{1}{2}$

Negative Numbers

Find the value of $|{}^-4|$.

Step 1: Find the distance from zero to the number inside the absolute value sign, ${}^-4$. You can find the distance by counting the number of units from 0 to ${}^-4$ on a number line.

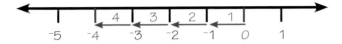

The distance is 4 units.

$$|{}^-4| = 4$$

Computations

Find the sum of $|{}^-2| + |5|$.

Step 1: To add absolute values, first find each absolute value.

> The absolute value of every negative number is the same as the number without the negative sign.
>
> $|{}^-8| = 8$ $|{}^-3.4| = 3.4$
>
> $\left|-\dfrac{2}{3}\right| = \dfrac{2}{3}$

$$|{}^-2| = 2 \qquad |5| = 5$$

Step 2: Write the problem using the absolute values.

$$|{}^-2| + |5|$$
$$2 + 5$$

Step 3: Add. $2 + 5 = 7$

Solve $|8 - 7|$.

Step 1: When the math problem is inside the absolute value sign, do the math first.
Subtract $8 - 7$.

$$|8 - 7|$$
$$|1|$$

Step 2: Find the absolute value.

$$|8 - 7| = 1$$

$$|1| = 1$$

Integers that have the same sign (+ or −) are called **like integers**.

Adding Positive Integers

Add ⁺16 + ⁺12.

Step 1: Positive integers are usually written without the positive sign. Write the problem without the positive signs.

$$^{+}16 + {}^{+}12$$
$$16 + 12$$

Step 2: Add the numbers.

$$16 + 12 = 28$$

Step 3: Since the problem uses the positive sign, put it back. The addends are positive, so the sum is also positive.

$$^{+}16 + {}^{+}12 = {}^{+}28$$

$$^{+}16 + {}^{+}12 = {}^{+}28$$

Kelly's puppy gained 4 ounces last week. It gained another 8 ounces this week. How much did the puppy's weight change over the two weeks?

Step 1: You can represent a gain using a positive number.

Last week: ⁺4
This week: ⁺8

Step 2: To find the change over both weeks, add the changes.

$$^{+}4 + {}^{+}8$$
$$4 + 8$$
$$4 + 8 = 12$$
$$^{+}4 + {}^{+}8 = {}^{+}12$$

Step 3: The problem asks how much the puppy's weight changed. The sum of the changes is ⁺12. A positive value is a gain.

Kelly's puppy gained 12 ounces.

Adding Two Negative Integers

Add $^-10 + ^-10$.

Step 1: Negative integers are added in the same way as positive. If both integers are negative, add the absolute values of the integers. Write the problem with no negative signs.

$$^-10 + ^-10$$
$$|^-10| + |^-10|$$
$$10 + 10$$

Step 2: Add $10 + 10$.

$$10 + 10 = 20$$

Step 3: Put the negative signs back. The addends are negative, so the sum is also negative.

$$^-10 + ^-10 = ^-20$$

$$^-10 + ^-10 = ^-20$$

addends—The numbers being added in an addition problem.

sum—The answer to an addition problem.

The Number Line

Use the number line to find $^-1 + ^-3$.

Step 1: Draw a number line.

Step 2: Begin at the first addend, $^-1$.

Step 3: When you add a positive number on a number line, you move right. Negatives are opposites of positives, so move the opposite direction, **left**. Move left 3 units. You end on $^-4$.

$$^-1 + ^-3 = ^-4$$

You will get the same answer if you solve using absolute values, then replace the negative sign.

$$^-1 + ^-3 = ?$$
$$|^-1| + |^-3| = ?$$
$$1 + 3 = 4$$
$$^-1 + ^-3 = ^-4$$

⑥ Addition: Unlike Integers

Integers that have different signs
(+ and −) are called **unlike integers.**

The Number Line

Use the number line to find ⁻2 + ⁺3.

Step 1: Begin at the first addend, ⁻2.

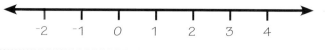

Step 2: When you add a positive number on a number line, you move right. Move right 3 units.

You end on ⁺1.

⁻2 + ⁺3 = ⁺1

Use a Picture

Use a picture to find ⁺2 + ⁻4.

Step 1: Draw a circle for each positive unit and an X for each negative unit.

Step 2: One negative unit cancels out one positive unit. Two negative units cancel out two positive units.

Step 3: Count what is left. There are two negative units left.   **⁺2 + ⁻4 = ⁻2**

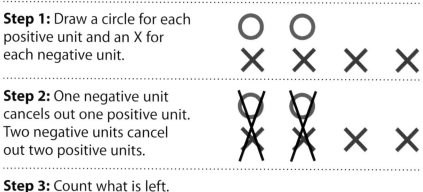

Sign of the Sum

When adding two numbers with different signs, the sum has the same sign as the number with the greatest absolute value.

$^-2 + {}^+3 = {}^+1$	$^+2 + {}^-4 = {}^-2$
$\lvert{}^-2\rvert = 2 \qquad \lvert{}^+3\rvert = 3$	$\lvert{}^+2\rvert = 2 \qquad \lvert{}^-4\rvert = 4$
$\lvert{}^-2\rvert < \lvert{}^+3\rvert$	$\lvert{}^+2\rvert < \lvert{}^-4\rvert$
$^+3$ has the greater absolute value.	$^-4$ has the greater absolute value.
The sum is **positive.**	The sum is **negative.**

Use Subtraction

In a football game, the Raiders lost 16 yards, then gained 58 yards. What was their total gain or loss?

Step 1: Use a negative integer to represent loss. Use a positive integer to represent gain.

16-yard loss	58-yard gain
$^-16$	$^+58$

Step 2: To find a total, add.

$$^-16 + {}^+58$$

Step 3: Unlike integers can be added by finding the difference of their absolute values. Subtract the smaller absolute value from the larger absolute value.

$$\lvert{}^-16\rvert = 16$$
$$\lvert{}^+58\rvert = 58$$

$$58 - 16 = 42$$

Step 4: The final answer has the same sign as the integer with the greater absolute value.

58 > 16, so the answer is positive.
$$^-16 + {}^+58 = {}^+42$$

The Raiders had a total gain of 42 yards.

⑦ Adding Rationals

All rational numbers (numbers that can be written as fractions) are added in the same way as integers.

Rational Addition

Adding rationals with the same sign:	$^-0.2 + {}^-0.5$
Add the absolute values.	$\lvert{}^-0.2\rvert + \lvert{}^-0.5\rvert$
The sum has the same sign as the addends.	$0.2 + 0.5 = 0.7$
	$^-0.2 + {}^-0.5 = {}^-0.7$
Adding rationals with different signs:	$^-2.7 + {}^+1.3$
Find the difference of the absolute values.	$\lvert{}^-2.7\rvert - \lvert{}^+1.3\rvert$
The sum has the same sign as the	$2.7 - 1.3 = 1.4$
rational with the greater absolute value.	$\lvert{}^-2.7\rvert > \lvert{}^+1.3\rvert$
	$^-2.7 + {}^+1.3 = {}^-1.4$

Like Rationals

Add $^-7.6 + {}^-0.2$.

Step 1: Add the absolute values by writing the problem with no negative signs.

$$^-7.6 + {}^-0.2$$
$$\lvert{}^-7.6\rvert + \lvert{}^-0.2\rvert$$
$$7.6 + 0.2$$

Step 2: Add.

$$\begin{array}{r} 7.6 \\ + 0.2 \\ \hline 7.8 \end{array}$$

Step 3: Put the negative signs back. $^-7.6 + {}^-0.2 = {}^-7.8$
The addends are negative, so the sum is also negative.

$^-7.6 + {}^-0.2 = {}^-7.8$

Unlike Rationals

Add $^+2\frac{1}{3} + ^-1\frac{1}{3}$.

Step 1: Unlike rationals are added by subtracting their absolute values. Subtract the smaller absolute value from the larger absolute value.

$$\left|^+2\frac{1}{3}\right| = 2\frac{1}{3}$$

$$\left|^-1\frac{1}{3}\right| = 1\frac{1}{3}$$

$$2\frac{1}{3} - 1\frac{1}{3} = 1$$

Step 2: The final answer has the same sign as the integer with the greater absolute value.

$2\frac{1}{3} > 1\frac{1}{3}$, **so the answer is positive.**

$$^+2\frac{1}{3} + ^-1\frac{1}{3} = ^+1$$

Adding Three or More Numbers

Marcia borrowed $8.42 from her dad. Then she paid him $7.00. She borrowed another $10.00. Then she paid him $11.00. Does she still owe her dad money? How much?

Step 1: Borrowing money can be represented by a negative number. Paying money back can be represented by a positive number.

Borrow	Pay
$^-8.42$	$^+7.00$
$^-10.00$	$^+11.00$

Step 2: Add the like numbers first.
Add the negative numbers.
Add the positive numbers.

$$^-8.42 + ^-10.00 = ^-18.42$$
$$^+7.00 + ^+11.00 = ^+18.00$$

Step 3: Now add the partial sums to find the total.
Subtract the absolute values.
The number with the greater absolute value is negative, so the sum is negative.

$$^-18.42 + ^+18.00$$
$$|^-18.42| + |^+18.00|$$
$$18.42 - 18.00 = 0.42$$

$$^-18.42 + ^+18.00 = ^-0.42$$

The sum is negative, so Marcia still owes her dad $0.42.

Addition Properties

There are four addition properties you can use to make solving addition problems easier.

Addition Properties

The Commutative Property: Changing the order of the addends does not change the sum.

$$a + b = b + a$$

The Associative Property: Changing the grouping of the addends does not change the sum.

$$(a + b) + c = a + (b + c)$$

The Zero Property: When you add zero and any number, the sum is that number.

$$a + 0 = a$$

The Inverse Property: When you add numbers that are opposites, the sum is zero.

$$a + (^-a) = 0$$

The Commutative Property

Show that $^-2.4 + {}^-1.3 = {}^-1.3 + {}^-2.4$

Step 1: Add $^-2.4 + {}^-1.3$.
Add the absolute values.
Put the negative signs back.

$$^-2.4 + {}^-1.3$$
$$|{}^-2.4| + |{}^-1.3|$$
$$2.4 + 1.3 = 3.7$$
$$^-2.4 + {}^-1.3 = {}^-3.7$$

Step 2: Add $^-1.3 + {}^-2.4$.
Add the absolute values.
Put the negative signs back.

$$^-1.3 + {}^-2.4$$
$$1.3 + 2.4 = 3.7$$
$$^-1.3 + {}^-2.4 = {}^-3.7$$

Step 3: Compare the sums.

$$^-2.4 + {}^-1.3 = {}^-3.7$$
$$^-1.3 + {}^-2.4 = {}^-3.7$$

The sums are the same, $^-3.7$.
Changing the order did not change the sum.

The Associative Property

Show that (⁻1 + ⁻2) + ⁺4 = ⁻1 + (⁻2 + ⁺4)

Step 1: Add (⁻1 + ⁻2) + ⁺4.
Always do the operation inside
parentheses first. ⁻1 + ⁻2 = ⁻3.
Add the remaining number.

$$(⁻1 + ⁻2) + ⁺4$$
$$(⁻3) \quad + ⁺4$$

$$(⁻3) + ⁺4 = ⁺1$$

Step 2: Add ⁻1 + (⁻2 + ⁺4).
Add inside the parentheses first.
⁻2 + ⁺4 = ⁺2.
Add the remaining number.

$$⁻1 + (⁻2 + ⁺4)$$
$$⁻1 + (⁺2)$$

$$⁻1 + (⁺2) = ⁺1$$

The sums are the same, ⁺1.
Changing the grouping did not change the sum.

The Zero Property

Add ⁻1.6 + 0.

Step 1: Add the absolute values. The absolute
value of 0 is 0. Since zero is neutral, use the
sign of the other number. The sum is negative.

$$⁻1.6 \ + 0$$
$$|⁻1.6| \ + \ |0|$$
$$1.6 \ + 0 = 1.6$$
$$⁻1.6 + 0 = ⁻1.6$$

Adding zero did not change the number.

The Inverse Property

Add ⁻9.7 + ⁺9.7.

Step 1: The numbers are unlike,
so subtract the absolute values.

$$⁻9.7 + ⁺9.7$$
$$|⁻9.7| - |⁺9.7|$$
$$9.7 - \ 9.7 = 0$$
$$⁻9.7 + ⁺9.7 = 0$$

**Adding opposite numbers
resulted in zero.**

Addition and subtraction are opposite operations. You can subtract an integer by adding the opposite integer.

Use a Number Line

Use the number line to find ⁻6 – ⁺2.

Step 1: Start at the first number, ⁻6.

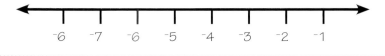

⁻6 ⁻7 ⁻6 ⁻5 ⁻4 ⁻3 ⁻2 ⁻1

Step 2: The second number tells you how many places to move.
Subtraction tells you to move the opposite way of addition.
Subtracting a positive number moves left.
Move left 2 places.

2   1
⁻8 ⁻7 ⁻6 ⁻5 ⁻4 ⁻3 ⁻2 ⁻1

You end on ⁻8.

⁻6 – ⁺2 = ⁻8

To **add** a **positive** number on the number line, move **right**.
To **subtract** a **positive** number on the number line, move **left**.

To **add** a **negative** number on the number line, move **left**.
To **subtract** a **negative** number on the number line, move **right**.

Add the Opposite

Subtract $^-12 - {}^-8$.

Step 1: You can subtract any number by adding its opposite. Write the first number.

$^-12 - {}^-8$
$^-12$

Step 2: Change the subtraction symbol to addition.

$^-12 +$

Step 3: Write the opposite of the second number. $^-12 + {}^+8$

Step 4: Add.

$^-12 + {}^+8 = {}^-4$

$^-12 - {}^-8 = {}^-4$

The highest point in California is Mount Whitney at 14,494 feet above sea level. The lowest point in California is in Death Valley at 282 feet below sea level. What is the difference in elevation?

Step 1: Distance above sea level is a positive number. Distance below sea level is a negative number.

	Elevation
Mount Whitney	$^+14,494$
Death Valley	$^-282$

Step 2: To find the difference, subtract. $^+14,494 - {}^-282$

Step 3: Add the opposite. Write the first number.

$^+14,494$

Step 4: Change the subtraction symbol to addition.

$^+14,494 +$

Step 5: Write the opposite of the second number.

$^+14,494 + {}^+282$

Step 6: Add.

$^+14,494 + {}^+282 = {}^+14,776$

There is an elevation difference of 14,776 feet between Mount Whitney and Death Valley.

⑩ Subtracting Rationals

To subtract a rational number, you can add the opposite rational number.

Rational Number Subtraction

1. Write the first rational number.
2. Change the subtraction sign to addition.
3. Write the opposite of the second number.
4. Add.

Subtracting Unlike Rationals

Subtract $^-\dfrac{3}{8} - {}^+\dfrac{1}{8}$.

Step 1: Write the first rational number.	$^-\dfrac{3}{8}$
Step 2: Change the subtraction sign to addition.	$^-\dfrac{3}{8} +$
Step 3: Write the opposite of the second number.	$^-\dfrac{3}{8} + {}^-\dfrac{1}{8}$
Step 4: Add.	$^-\dfrac{3}{8} + {}^-\dfrac{1}{8} = {}^-\dfrac{4}{8}$
Step 5: Reduce the fraction to lowest terms.	$^-\dfrac{4}{8} = {}^-\dfrac{1}{2}$

$$^-\dfrac{3}{8} - {}^+\dfrac{1}{8} = {}^-\dfrac{1}{2}$$

Change subtraction of **unlike** rationals to addition of **like** rationals.

24

Subtracting Like Rationals
Subtract $^-208.7 - {}^-22.4$

> Change subtraction of like rationals to addition of **unlike** rationals.

Step 1: Write the first rational. $^-208.7$

Step 2: Change the subtraction $^-208.7 +$ symbol to addition.

Step 3: Write the opposite of $^-208.7 + {}^+22.4$ the second number.

Step 4: Add. Remember, to add $|^-208.7| - |^+22.4|$
unlike rationals, subtract $208.7 - 22.4 = 186.3$
the absolute values. Keep the $^-208.7 + {}^+22.4 = {}^-186.3$
sign of the number with
the greater absolute value. $^-208.7 - {}^-22.4 = {}^-186.3$

Add a Negative or Subtract a Positive?
Bruce has $10. He spends $3. To find what he has left, should you subtract $10 – $3, or add $10 + ⁻$3?

Step 1: Can you use a subtraction problem? $\$10 - \$3 = \$7$
Bruce started with some money, then
took some away. So, yes, you can subtract.

Step 2: Can you use an addition problem? $^+\$10 + {}^-\$3 = \$7$
Bruce has a positive cash balance ($^+\$10$).
He spends some, which is   **You can choose which**
represented as a negative ($^-\$3$).   **way to solve the problem.**
To find a total left, you can add.   **The results are the same.**

Why Add a Negative?
Subtraction does not have the same properties as addition.

$10 - 7$ is not the same as $7 - 10$.

$3 \qquad \neq \qquad {}^-3$

When you write a subtraction problem as addition, you can use the addition properties.

$10 + {}^-7$ is the same as $^-7 + 10$.

$3 \qquad \neq \qquad 3$

Integer multiplication is similar to whole number multiplication. The only difference is knowing if the answer is positive or negative.

Multiplying with Negatives

Let's say you're playing a game with circles.

$^+10$ $^-10$

Blue circles are each worth $^+10$.   Red circles are each worth $^-10$.

If you gain 3 blue circles, the value
of your circles changes by $3 \times {}^+10$, or $^+30$.

$$^+3 \times {}^+10 = {}^+30$$

A positive times a positive is positive.

$$+ \times\ + =\ +$$

If you gain 3 red circles, the value
of your circles change by $3 \times {}^-10$, or $^-30$.

$$^+3 \times {}^-10 = {}^-30$$

A positive times a negative is negative.

$$+ \times\ - =\ -$$

If you lose 3 blue circles, the value
of your circles changes by $^-3 \times {}^+10$, or $^-30$.

$$^-3 \times {}^+10 = {}^-30$$

A negative times a positive is negative.

$$- \times\ + =\ -$$

If you lose 3 red circles, the value of
your circles changes by $^-3 \times {}^-10$, or $^+30$.

$$^-3 \times {}^-10 = {}^+30$$

By getting rid of negatives,

$$- \times\ - =\ +$$

the total value goes up.

A negative times a negative is positive.

Multiplying Like Integers

Multiply ⁻6 × ⁻5.

Step 1: Pretend the signs are not there.

$$⁻6 × ⁻5 \quad \diagup 6 × \diagup 5$$

Step 2: Multiply.

$$6 × 5 = 30$$

Step 3: Place the sign. When two factors have the same sign, the product is positive.

$$⁻6 × ⁻5 = ⁺30$$

> Numbers being multiplied are called **factors**. The answer to a multiplication problem is called a **product**.

Multiplying Unlike Integers

A stock value changes by ⁻3 points each day for 8 days. What is the total change after the 8 days?

Step 1: Multiply ⁻3 × ⁺8. Pretend the signs are not there.

$$⁻3 × ⁺8 \quad \diagup 3 × \diagup 8$$

Step 2: Multiply.

$$3 × 8 = 24$$

Step 3: Place the sign. When two factors have different signs, the product is negative.

$$⁻3 × ⁺8 = ⁻24$$

The total change in the stock value is ⁻24 points.

NO!

Multiplying Rationals

Multiplying rational numbers follows the same rules as multiplying integers.

Multiplication Rules

1. When two factors have the same sign, the product is positive.

> **positive × positive = positive**
>
> **negative × negative = positive**

2. When two factors have different signs, the product is negative.

> **positive × negative = negative**
>
> **negative × positive = negative**

Like Rationals

Multiply $^+3 \times {}^+\frac{1}{6}$.

Step 1: Pretend the signs are not there.

$$^+3 \times {}^+\frac{1}{6} \qquad {}^+\cancel{3} \times {}^+\frac{\cancel{1}}{6}$$

Step 2: Multiply. To multiply a whole number and a fraction, first write the whole number as a fraction.

$$3 = \frac{3}{1}$$

Multiply the numerators. Multiply the denominators. Reduce.

$$\frac{3}{1} \times \frac{1}{6} = \frac{3 \times 1}{1 \times 6} = \frac{3}{6} = \frac{1}{2}$$

Step 3: Place the sign. Both factors are positive, so the product is positive.

$$^+3 \times {}^+\frac{1}{6} = {}^+\frac{1}{2}$$

Unlike Rationals

Charles has a lunch card that debits his account by $1.75 every time he buys a school lunch. What is the difference in his account if he buys 4 lunches?

Step 1: A debit to an account is a negative value. Multiply the debit amount (⁻$1.75) by the number of times the card was used.

−$1.75 × 4

Step 2: Pretend the signs are not there. −$1.75 × 4   ⟋$1.75 × 4

Step 3: Multiply.

$$\begin{array}{r} 1.75 \\ \times\ \ 4 \\ \hline 7.00 \end{array}$$

Step 4: Place the sign. One factor is negative and one is positive, so the product is negative.

−$1.75 × 4 = −$7.00

Charles's account is different by −$7.00.

Sign Busting Tip:
When you multiply more than two numbers, count the negative signs.
An **even** number of negative signs means the product is **positive**.

$$(^-1) \times (^-1) \times (^+1) \times (^-1) \times (^-1) = {}^+1$$
$$\ \ 1 \quad\ \ \ 2 \qquad\qquad\ \ 3 \quad\ \ 4$$

An **odd** number of negative signs means the product is **negative**.

$$(^-1) \times (^+1) \times (^-1) \times (^-1) = {}^-1$$
$$\ \ 1 \qquad\qquad\ 2 \quad\ \ 3$$

Multiplication
Properties

Multiplication has some of
the same properties as addition.

Multiplication Properties

The Commutative Property:
Changing the order of the factors
does not change the product.

$$a \times b = b \times a$$
$$4 \times 3 = 3 \times 4$$
$$12 = 12$$

The Associative Property:
Changing the grouping of the
factors does not change the product.

$$(a \times b) \times c = a \times (b \times c)$$
$$(1 \times 2) \times 3 = 1 \times (2 \times 3)$$
$$(2) \quad \times 3 = 1 \times \quad (6)$$
$$6 = 6$$

The Zero Property: When you
multiply zero and any number,
the product is always zero.

$$0 \times a = 0$$
$$0 \times {}^-6 = 0$$
$$0 \times 12 = 0$$

The Identity Property: When you
multiply one and any number,
the product is always that other number.

$$1 \times a = a$$
$$1 \times {}^-4 = {}^-4$$
$$1 \times 300 = 300$$

The Inverse Property: When you
multiply a number and its
inverse, the product is always one.
(See page 31 for more on inverses.)

$$a \times \frac{1}{a} = 1$$
$$8 \times \frac{1}{8} = 1$$

The Commutative Property

Does ⁻2 × 3 have the same product as 3 × ⁻2?

Step 1: Multiply ⁻2 × 3.
Pretend the signs are not there.
Multiply. Place the sign.
The signs are unlike, so the product is negative.

$$⁻2 × 3$$
$$2 × 3 = 6$$
$$⁻2 × 3 = ⁻6$$

Step 2: Multiply 3 × ⁻2.
Pretend the signs are not there.
Multiply. Place the sign.
The signs are unlike, so the product is negative.

$$3 × ⁻2$$
$$3 × 2 = 6$$
$$⁻3 × ⁻2 = ⁻6$$

Yes, ⁻2 × 3 has the same product as 3 × ⁻2, ⁻6.

What Is an Inverse?

When you invert something, you turn it upside down.

The **inverse** of a rational number is the rational number turned upside down.

The inverse of $\frac{2}{3}$ is $\frac{3}{2}$.   **The inverse of 4, or $\frac{4}{1}$, is $\frac{1}{4}$.**

The inverse of a number is also called its **reciprocal**.
Inverse numbers, or reciprocals, always have a product of 1.

The Inverse Property

Multiply ⁻6 × ⁻$\frac{1}{6}$.

Step 1: Pretend the signs are not there.

$$⁺6 × ⁻\frac{1}{6}$$

$$6 × \frac{1}{6}$$

Step 2: Multiply.

$$\frac{6}{1} × \frac{1}{6} = \frac{6 × 1}{1 × 6} × \frac{6}{6} = 1$$

Step 3: Place the sign. The signs are like, so the product is positive.

$$⁻6 × ⁻\frac{1}{6} = 1$$

⑭ The Distributive Property

The distributive property uses multiplication and addition together.

The Distributive Property

Any number can be written as a sum of two other numbers. For example, 8 can be written as (5 + 3) or (10 + ⁻2).

In a multiplication problem, sometimes one of the factors is written as a sum. You can add, then multiply, or you can multiply each addend separately, then add the products. The answer is the same.

$$7 \times (10 + {}^-2) \text{ is the same as } (7 \times 10) + (7 \times {}^-2)$$

7 ×	8		70	+	⁻14
	56			56	

Mental Math

Solve 3 × 53 using mental math.

Step 1: You can use the distributive property to solve problems mentally.

Think: **3 × 53 is the same as 3 × (50 + 3). I can multiply 3 × 50 and 3 × 3. Then I can add the products.**
$$3 \times 53 = 3 \times (50 + 3)$$
$$= (3 \times 50) + (3 \times 3)$$

Step 2: Think: **3 × 50 = 150   3 × 3 = 9**

Step 3: Think: **150 + 9 = 159**
3 × 53 = 159

Using the Distributive Property

Solve (4.8 × 22) + (5.2 × 22).

This problem can be solved in more than one way.

One way:

Step 1: Multiply 4.8 × 22.

$$\begin{array}{r} 4.8 \\ \times 22 \\ \hline 96 \\ +960 \\ \hline 105.6 \end{array}$$

(4.8 × 22) + (5.2 × 22)
(105.6) + (5.2 × 22)

Step 2: Multiply 5.2 × 22.

$$\begin{array}{r} 5.2 \\ \times 22 \\ \hline 104 \\ +1040 \\ \hline 114.4 \end{array}$$

(105.6) + (5.2 × 22)
(105.6) + (114.4)

Step 3: Add 105.6 + 114.4.

$$\begin{array}{r} 105.6 \\ +114.4 \\ \hline 220.0 \end{array}$$

105.6 + 114.4 = 220

> The distributive property can also be used with multiplication and subtraction.
>
> 3 × (10 – 4) = (3 × 10) – (3 × 4)

Another way:

Step 1: You can use the distributive property to combine numbers that are multiplied by the same factor.

In this problem, 4.8 and 5.2 are each multiplied by 22.
The distributive property says

(4.8 × 22) + (5.2 × 22)

(4.8 × 22) + (5.2 × 22) = (4.8 + 5.2) × 22

Step 2: Add 4.8 + 5.2.

(4.8 + 5.2) × 22
10   × 22

Step 3: Multiply.

10 × 22 = 220

(4.8 × 22) + (5.2 × 22) = 220
Both ways have the same result, 220.

All rationals, including integers, are divided as positive numbers.
The sign in the answer is found in the same way as it is for multiplication.

Division Rules

1. The quotient of two numbers with the same sign is positive.

positive ÷ positive = positive

negative ÷ negative = positive

2. The quotient of two numbers with different signs is negative.

positive ÷ negative = negative

negative ÷ positive = negative

Dividing Like Integers

Divide $^-21 \div {}^-3$.

Step 1: Pretend the signs are not there.　　$^-21 \div {}^-3 \nearrow 21 \div \nearrow 3$

Step 2: Divide.　　$21 \div 3 = 7$

Step 3: Place the sign. The signs are like, so the quotient is positive.　　$^-21 \div {}^-3 = {}^+7$

The number being divided is the **dividend**.
The number being divided by is the **divisor**.
The answer to a division problem is the **quotient**.
dividend ÷ divisor = quotient

Dividing Unlike Integers

Divide $^-40 \div {}^+10$.

Step 1: Pretend the signs are not there. $^-40 \div {}^+10$ $\not{}^-40 \div \not{}^+10$

Step 2: Divide. $40 \div 10 = 4$

Step 3: Place the sign.
The signs are different, so
the quotient is negative. $^-40 \div {}^+10 = {}^-4$

Dividing Like Rationals

Divide $^+\dfrac{2}{9} \div {}^+\dfrac{1}{3}$.

Step 1: Pretend the signs are not there. $^+\dfrac{2}{9} \div {}^+\dfrac{1}{3}$ $\not{}^+\dfrac{2}{9} \div \not{}^+\dfrac{1}{3}$

Step 2: Fractions are divided by
multiplying by the reciprocal. $\dfrac{2}{9} \div \dfrac{1}{3} = \dfrac{2}{9} \times \dfrac{3}{1}$
Change the division sign to a multiplication sign.
Flip the second fraction upside down
to multiply by the reciprocal.

Step 3: Multiply. $\dfrac{2}{\underset{3}{\cancel{9}}} \times \dfrac{\overset{1}{\cancel{3}}}{1} = \dfrac{2 \times 1}{3 \times 1} = \dfrac{2}{3}$

Step 4: Place the sign.
The signs are the same, $^+\dfrac{2}{9} \div {}^+\dfrac{1}{3} = {}^+\dfrac{2}{3}$
so the quotient is positive.

Dividing Unlike Rationals

Divide $^+1.5 \div {}^-3$.

Step 1: Pretend the signs are not there. $^+1.5 \div {}^-3$ $\not{}^+1.5 \div \not{}^-3$

Step 2: Divide. $\begin{array}{r} 0.5 \\ 3\overline{)1.5} \end{array}$

Step 3: Place the sign. $^+1.5 \div {}^-3 = {}^-0.5$
The signs are different, so the quotient is negative.

Variables *and* Expressions

Numbers, letters, and operation
symbols are used in algebra
to replace words.

Expressions, Operations, and Variables

An **expression** stands for a number. An expression can be a
number, like 600. An expression can also be a letter, like *t*,
that stands for an unknown number. Or an expression can show
a number using an operation, like $9 - 3$.

Numbers in an expression are called **constants**, because they
do not change. Letters, called **variables**, are used to represent
numbers that are unknown or that change.

Numeric expressions do not use variables. Expressions that use
a variable are called **algebraic expressions.** Word expressions
can be written as numeric or algebraic expressions.

To write a word expression as a numeric or algebraic expression,
write a number when one is given. Write a variable when you
don't know a number. Use an operation symbol when you see
words like plus (+), minus (−), times (×), or divided by (÷).

Word Expression	Numeric or Algebraic Expression
seven plus twelve	$7 + 12$
six minus a number	$6 - n$
money in your wallet	m
a distance divided by ten	$d \div 10$

36

Numeric Expressions

Five girls joined three other girls on a bike ride. Write an expression for the total number of girls on the bike ride.

Step 1: Write *five girls joined three girls* using numbers and symbols. The word *joined* tells you this is addition.

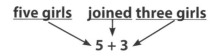

five girls   joined three girls

5 + 3

Algebraic Expressions

Write an algebraic expression for "twenty times the number of students in a group."

The symbol for multiplication, x, is easy to confuse with the letter x. In algebra, when there is no symbol, multiplication is understood.

5c means "5 multiplied by c."

Step 1: The number of students in your group is unknown. Choose a letter to represent the unknown. You can use the first letter of a word as a variable to help you remember what the variable represents.

s = **number of students in a group**

Step 2: Replace words with numbers, symbols, and variables.

twenty times the number of students in a group

20   × s

$20 \times s$, or $20s$

17 Evaluate and Simplify

Expressions can be written in different ways without changing their value.

Numeric Expressions

Evaluate the expression 9 × 6.

Step 1: *Evaluate* means "find the value of." To evaluate a numeric expression, do the operations in the expression to get a single number.

Multiply. $9 \times 6 = 54$

Algebraic Expressions

Evaluate the expression x + 8 when x = 3.

Step 1: Find the value of the expression by replacing the variables with numbers. Replace *x* with the number 3.

$x + 8$
$3 + 8$

Step 2: Add. $3 + 8 = 11$

When $x = 3$, $x + 8 = 11$.

Evaluate or Simplify?

evaluate—Find the value of.

simplify—Make simpler.

Problems that ask you to evaluate or simplify expressions may be asking you to do the same thing.

Usually evaluating an expression gives a numeric answer.

Simplifying an expression might have a numeric answer, or it might have an answer that is a simpler algebraic expression.

Coefficients and Like Terms

The **terms** of an expression are the parts that are separated by an addition or subtraction sign.

In the expression $8 + 3$, the terms are 8 and 3.

In the algebraic expression $2a - 3b$, the terms are $2a$ and $3b$.

In a term with a number and a variable, like $2a$, the number is called the **coefficient**. The coefficient is multiplied by the variable. $2a$ means 2 times a.

$$2a$$

coefficient   variable

When a term is a variable by itself, the coefficient is 1.

x is the same as **$1x$**

Terms that have exactly the same variables are called **like terms**.

$5a$ and $2a$ are like terms. $3ab$ and $2a$ are not like terms.

Simplifying Algebraic Expressions

Simplify the expression 2x + 9x.

Step 1: The distributive property lets you combine like terms. (See page 32.)

$2x + 9x$
$(2 + 9)x$

Step 2: Add inside the parentheses.

$11x$

$2x + 9x = 11x$

There are 5 full boxes of crayons. Two boxes are accidently left outside and melt in the sun.
If c represents the number of crayons in each box, then the expression (5c – 2c) can be used to represent the total number of crayons left. Simplify the expression 5c – 2c.

Step 1: You can combine like terms without writing out the distributive property.
Just add or subtract the coefficients. $5 - 2 = 3$.

$5c - 2c$
$3c$

$5c - 2c = 3c$

39

Order of Operations

The expression 12 + 6 ÷ (9 − 3) has three operations. How do you decide which operation to do first?

Order of Operations

The **order of operations** is a set of rules that tells you which operations to do first.

1. Do operations inside **parentheses**.
2. Do **multiplication and division** in order from left to right.
3. Do **addition and subtraction** in order from left to right.

Using the Order of Operations

Evaluate the expression 12 + 6 ÷ (9 − 3).

Step 1: Follow the order of operations. Do operations inside parentheses first. Subtract. 9 − 3 = 6.

$$12 + 6 ÷ (9 − 3)$$
$$12 + 6 ÷ (6)$$

Step 2: Do multiplication and division. There is a division sign. Divide. 6 ÷ 6 = 1.

$$12 + 6 ÷ 6$$
$$12 + 1$$

Step 3: Do addition and subtraction. There is an addition sign. Add. 12 + 1 = 13.

$$12 + 1$$
$$13$$
$$12 + 6 ÷ (9 − 3) = 13$$

What happens if *you do not follow the rules?* Do the operations straight from left to right, ignoring the parentheses.

$$12 + 6 ÷ (9 − 3)$$
$$18 ÷ 9 − 3$$
$$2 − 3$$
$$− 1$$

The answer is wrong.

<u>Follow</u> <u>the</u> <u>rules</u> to get the right answer!

Multiply with Variables

Let the variable b stand for the
amount of water in one bucket.
$2b$ is the amount of water in 2 buckets.

$2b$

To represent 3 times the amount of water in 2 buckets, you can
add $2b$ three times ($2b + 2b + 2b$), or you can multiply $3 \times 2b$.

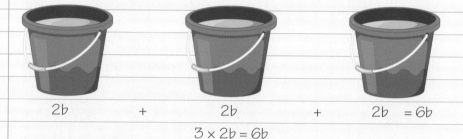

| $2b$ | + | $2b$ | + | $2b$ | $= 6b$ |

$3 \times 2b = 6b$

To multiply a number (like 3) and an algebraic term (like $2b$),
multiply the numbers and keep the variable the same.

$$3 \times 2b = 3 \times 2 \times b = 6b$$

Simplifying Algebraic Expressions

Use the order of operations to simplify $a + 3 \times (8a – 2a)$.

Step 1: Do the operations inside
parentheses first. $8a – 2a = 6a$.

$a + 3 \times (8a – 2a)$
$a + 3 \times (6a)$
$a + 3 \times 6a$

Step 2: Multiply and divide.
There is a multiplication sign.
Multiply. $3 \times 6a = 18a$.

$a + 3 \times 6a$
$a + 18a$

Step 3: Add and subtract.
There is an addition sign,
and the terms are like terms.
Add. $a + 18a = 19a$.
You are finished.

$a + 18a$
$19a$

> a is the
> same as $1a$.
> $a + 18a$
> is the same as
> $1a + 18a$.

$a + 3 \times (8a – 2a) = 19a$

41

⑲ Algebraic Equations

Algebraic equations connect
two expressions using an equal sign.

Writing an Equation

Write an equation for the following sentence: Sally's age plus three years is 19.

Step 1: Choose a letter to represent the unknown (Sally's age).

$$s = \text{Sally's age}$$

Step 2: Replace the words in the sentence with numbers, symbols, and variables. The word *is* means "equals."

Sally's age plus three years is 19.

$$s + 3 = 19$$

> Algebra replaces empty boxes, or blank spaces, with variables.
> $\square + 3 = 19$ becomes
> $s + 3 = 19$

Expression or Equation?

An **expression** is a phrase. It is not a full thought.

"Sally's age plus three years" is a phrase, but does not tell you anything.

expression   expression

$$\underline{s + 3} \quad = \quad \underline{19}$$

equation

An **equation** is a sentence. It is a full thought. The sentence "Sally's age plus three years is nineteen" is a full thought. It tells you something about Sally's age.

Algebraic equations use an equal sign to connect expressions.

Evaluating Equations

When you evaluate an equation, you decide if the equation is true or false for the given value.

Evaluate the equation 30r = 140 when r = 3.

Step 1: Replace the variable, *r*, with the given value, 3.

$$30r = 140$$
$$30(3) = 140$$

Step 2: Multiply. 30 × 3 = 90.

$$90 = 140$$

Step 3: Compare the left and right sides of the equation. Are they same? No. **30r = 140 is not true for r = 3.**

The **solution** to an equation is the number, or set of numbers, that makes the equation true. The solution to $2 + a = 3$ is $a = 1$.

Solving Equations

Kendra has 28 freckles on her nose. She also has 50 freckles on her cheeks. To find the total number of freckles, solve the equation 28 + 50 = f.

Step 1: When you solve an equation, you find the value that makes the equation true. What value for *f* will make this equation true? Add the numbers on the left side of the equal sign.

$$28 + 50 = f$$
$$78 = f$$

Step 2: Compare the left and right sides of the equation. The only number for *f* that will make the equation true is 78. Write the solution.

f = 78
Kendra has 78 freckles.

When you do the same operation on each side of an equation, the equation is still true.

The Seesaw

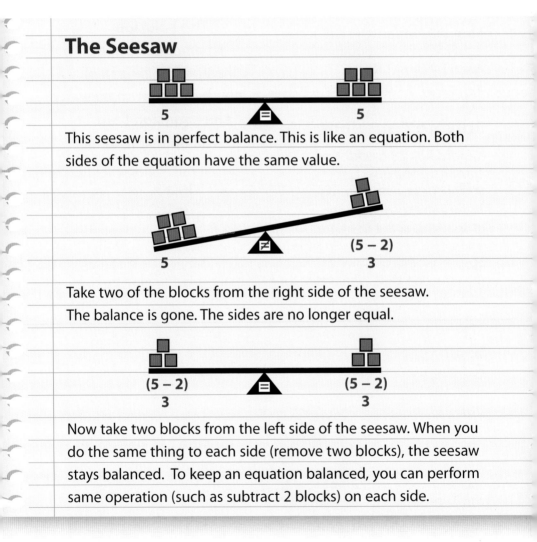

This seesaw is in perfect balance. This is like an equation. Both sides of the equation have the same value.

Take two of the blocks from the right side of the seesaw. The balance is gone. The sides are no longer equal.

Now take two blocks from the left side of the seesaw. When you do the same thing to each side (remove two blocks), the seesaw stays balanced. To keep an equation balanced, you can perform same operation (such as subtract 2 blocks) on each side.

Properties of Equality

addition property of equality—You can **add** the same value to both sides of an equation and the equation will still be true.

subtraction property of equality—You can **subtract** the same value from both sides of an equation and it will still be true.

multiplication property of equality—You can **multiply** both sides of an equation by the same value and it will still be true.

division property of equality—You can **divide** both sides of an equation by the same value and it will still be true.

The Addition Property of Equality

Is the equation 6 − 4 = 2 still true when you add 20 to each side of the equal sign?

Step 1: Write the original equation. $\quad\quad 6 - 4 = 2$

Step 2: Add 20 to each side. $\quad\quad (6 - 4) + 20 = 2 + 20$

Step 3: Do the operations. $\quad\quad\quad\quad 22 = 22$

Yes, the equation is still true.

The Multiplication Property of Equality

Is the equation 8 + 4 = 12 still true when you multiply the expression on each side of the equal sign by 2?

Step 1: Write the original equation. $\quad\quad 8 + 4 = 12$

Step 2: Multiply each side of the equal sign by 2. Use parentheses to be sure you multiply the entire expression on each side, and not just one term. $\quad (8 + 4) \times 2 = 12 \times 2$

Step 3: Do the operations.

$$(8 + 4) \times 2 = 12 \times 2$$
$$(12) \quad \times 2 = 12 \times 2$$
$$24 = 24$$

Yes, the equation is still true.

21 Addition Equations

It's easy to solve equations with variables. Just get the variable by itself on one side of the equal sign.

Solving Addition Equations

Solve d + 16 = 28.

Step 1: Write the equation. $d + 16 = 28$

Step 2: Get the variable, d, by itself on one side of the equation. Remember, you can perform the same operation on each side of an equal sign, and the equation is still true.

When a number is added to a variable (+ 16), use the inverse operation, subtraction (− 16), to get the variable by itself.

Subtract 16 from each side of the equation. $d + 16 - 16 = 28 - 16$

Step 3: Do the operations. Adding 16 and subtracting 16 cancel each other out (16 − 16 = 0).
$$d + \cancel{16} - \cancel{16} = 28 - 16$$
$$d = 12$$

28 − 16 = 12
$$d = 12$$

> **Inverse operations** do the opposite of each other.
>
> Addition and subtraction are inverse operations.

Check the Solution

Check the solution to the equation above.

Step 1: Write the original equation. $d + 16 = 28$

Step 2: Replace the variable, d, with the solution, 12. $12 + 16 = 28$

Step 3: Do the operations. Are the expressions on both sides of the equal sign the same? Yes. $28 = 28$

For the equation $d + 16 = 28$, the solution $d = 12$ is correct.

Addition Word Problems

Harry bought a movie ticket and a $5.00 popcorn. He spent a total of $12.75. Write an algebraic equation and solve it to find the cost of the movie ticket.

Step 1: Use a word equation to show what the problem is saying.

cost of movie ticket plus $5.00 is $12.75

Step 2: Choose a variable for the value you don't know.

Let m = cost of a movie ticket.

Step 3: Replace words with numbers, symbols, and variables.

cost of movie ticket plus $5.00 is $12.75

$$m + \$5.00 = \$12.75$$

Step 4: This is an addition problem. Get the variable, m, by itself using subtraction. Subtract $5.00 from each side of the equation. Instead of rewriting the entire equation, you can write the inverse operation below the equation on each side.

$$m + \$5.00 = \$12.75$$
$$- \$5.00 \quad - \$5.00$$

Step 5: Do the operations. Adding $5.00 and subtracting $5.00 cancel each other out. $12.75 − $5.00 = $7.75

$$m + \cancel{\$5.00} = \$12.75$$
$$\underline{- \cancel{\$5.00} \quad - \$5.00}$$
$$m \qquad\quad = \$7.75$$

$m = \$7.75$

Step 6: Check the solution. Write the original equation. Replace the variable, *m*, with the solution, $7.75. Add. Both sides of the equal sign are the same, so the solution is correct.

$$m + \$5.00 = \$12.75$$
$$\$7.75 + \$5.00 = \$12.75$$
$$\$12.75 = \$12.75$$

The cost of Harry's movie ticket was $7.75.

㉒ Subtraction Equations

The inverse of subtraction is addition. Use addition to get the variable by itself in a subtraction equation.

Solving Subtraction Equations

Solve n − 4 = 16. Check your solution.

Step 1: Write the equation.

$$n - 4 = 16$$

Step 2: Get the variable, *n*, by itself. When a number is subtracted from a variable, use addition to get the variable by itself. Add 4 to each side of the equation.

$$\begin{array}{r} n - 4 = 16 \\ +4 \quad +4 \end{array}$$

Step 3: Do the operations. Subtracting 4 and adding 4 cancel each other out. 16 + 4 = 20

$$\begin{array}{r} n - \cancel{4} = 16 \\ +\cancel{4} \quad +4 \\ \hline n \quad\quad = 20 \end{array}$$

Step 4: Check the solution. Write the original equation. Replace the variable, *n*, with the solution, 20. Subtract. The solution is correct.

$$\begin{aligned} n - 4 &= 16 \\ 20 - 4 &= 16 \\ 16 &= 16 \\ n &= 20 \end{aligned}$$

Negative Numbers

Solve y − ⁻12 = 10. Check your solution.

Step 1: Write the equation.

$$y - {}^-12 = 10$$

Step 2: Get the variable, *y*, by itself using addition. Since the number being subtracted is negative, add a negative number (⁻12) to each side.

$$\begin{array}{r} y - {}^-12 = \quad 10 \\ +{}^-12 \quad +{}^-12 \end{array}$$

Step 3: Do the operations. 10 + −12 = −2

$$\begin{array}{r} \dfrac{y - \cancel{{}^-12}}{+\cancel{{}^-12}} = \dfrac{10}{+{}^-12} \\ y \quad\quad = \quad {}^-2 \end{array}$$

Step 4: Check the solution.
Write the original equation.
Replace the variable, y, with the
solution, $^-2$. Subtract.
The solution is correct.

$$y - {}^-12 = 10$$
$$^-2 - {}^-12 = 10$$
$$^-2 + {}^+12 = 10$$
$$10 = 10$$

Subtraction Word Problems

*Danika gave her science teacher
27 beetles from her insect collection.
She has 314 insects left. Write and
solve an algebraic equation to find
how many insects she had before
she gave away the beetles.*

To subtract,
add the opposite.

$$2 - {}^-1$$

is the same as

$$2 + {}^+1.$$

Step 1: Use a word equation
to show what the problem is saying.

original insects minus beetles given away equals insects left

Step 2: Replace words with numbers, symbols, and variables,
using a variable for the value you don't know.

Let i = original number of insects

original insects minus beetles given away equals insects left

$$i - 27 = 314$$

Step 3: This is a subtraction problem.
Use addition to get the variable by itself.

$$i - 27 = 314$$
$$+ 27 \quad + 27$$

Step 4: Do the operations.

$$i - 27 = 314$$
$$+27 \quad + 27$$
$$i \quad\quad = 341$$

Step 5: Check the solution.
Write the original equation.
Replace the variable with
the solution. Subtract.
The solution is correct.

$$i - 27 = 314$$
$$341 - 27 = 314$$
$$314 = 314$$

**Danika had 341 insects before
she gave away the beetles.**

Multiplication

Equations

Use division to solve multiplication equations that have a variable.

Solving Multiplication Equations

Solve 8k = 56.

Step 1: Write the equation.

$$8k = 56$$

Step 2: Get the variable, *k*, by itself. When a variable is multiplied by a number, use division to get the variable by itself. Divide each side of the equation by the coefficient, 8. Use a fraction bar to show division.

$$\frac{8k}{8} = \frac{56}{8}$$

Step 3: Do the operations.

$$56 \div 8 = 7$$
$$\frac{\cancel{8}k}{\cancel{8}} = \frac{56}{8}$$
$$k = 7$$

Step 4: Check the solution.

$$8k = 56$$
$$8(7) = 56$$
$$56 = 56$$

$$k = 7$$

> **Remember:**
> The coefficient is the number part of an algebraic term.
>
> $$\overset{\frown}{8k}$$
> coefficient variable

> **Multiplication and division are inverse operations.**
>
> They do the opposite of each other.

Multiplication Word Problems

One ride ticket at the fair costs $0.75. The total cost for the Tilt-A-Whirl ride is $3.75. How many tickets are needed for this ride?

Step 1: Use a word equation to show what the problem is saying.

cost of ride equals price of one ticket times number of tickets

Step 2: Replace words with numbers, symbols, and variables, using a variable for the value you don't know.

Let t = number of tickets.

cost of ride equals price of one ticket times number of tickets

$$\$3.75 = \$0.75t$$

Step 3: This is a multiplication problem. Get the variable by itself. Divide both sides of the equation by the coefficient, $0.75.

$$\frac{\$3.75}{\$0.75} = \frac{\$0.75t}{\$0.75}$$

Step 4: Do the operations.
$3.75 \div \$0.75 = 5$

$$\frac{\$3.75}{\$0.75} = \frac{\cancel{\$0.75}t}{\cancel{\$0.75}}$$

$$5 = t$$

$t = 5$

Step 5: Check the solution.

$$\$3.75 = \$0.75t$$
$$\$3.75 = \$0.75(5)$$
$$\$3.75 = \$3.75$$

The solution is correct.

$t = 5$
The ride takes 5 tickets.

Division Equations

24

Some math problems divide a variable by a number. Others divide a number by a variable. You can solve both using multiplication.

Variable as the Dividend

Solve $\frac{x}{3} = 20$. Check your solution.

Step 1: Write the equation. Division in algebra is usually written using the fraction bar.
In this equation, the variable is the dividend, or the number being divided.

$$\frac{x}{3} = 20$$

Step 2: Get the variable, x, by itself. Since the variable is being divided by 3, multiply both sides of the equation by 3.

$$\frac{x}{3}(3) = 20(3)$$

Step 3: Multiply.
$20 \times 3 = 60$

$$\frac{x}{3}(3) = 20(3)$$
$$\frac{x}{3}\left(\frac{\cancel{3}}{1}\right) = 20(3)$$
$$x = 60$$

Step 4: Check the solution.
The solution is correct.
$x = 60$

$$\frac{x}{3} = 20$$
$$\frac{60}{3} = 20$$
$$20 = 20$$

> Parentheses can be used to show multiplication.
> 20(3) means 20 x 3

Variable as the Divisor

Solve $\dfrac{1.6}{y} = 8$. Check your solution.

Step 1: Write the equation. In this equation, the variable is the divisor, or the number something is divided by.

$$\frac{1.6}{y} = 8$$

Step 2: To get the variable, y, by itself takes two steps. First, multiply both sides of the equation by the variable.

$$\frac{1.6}{y}(y) = 8y$$

$$\frac{1.6}{\cancel{y}}\left(\frac{\cancel{y}}{1}\right) = 8y$$

$$1.6 = 8y$$

Step 3: Now this is a multiplication problem. To get y by itself, divide by the coefficient (8) of the new term, $8y$.
$1.6 \div 8 = 0.2$

$$\frac{1.6}{8} = \frac{8y}{8}$$

$$0.2 = y$$

Step 4: Check the solution.
The solution is correct.

$y = 0.2$

$$\frac{1.6}{y} = 8$$

$$\frac{1.6}{0.2} = 8$$

$$8 = 8$$

Division and Multiplication

Since division and multiplication are inverse operations, any division problem can be written as a multiplication problem.

The problem above says
1.6 divided by some number equals 8.

$$\frac{1.6}{y} = 8$$

In step 2, the problem is rewritten as multiplication.
1.6 equals 8 multiplied by some number.

$$1.6 = 8y$$

Multi-Step Problems

Problems with more than one operation
use more than one step to find a solution.

More Than One Operation

When a problem has only one operation,
it is solved by getting the variable by itself
on one side of the equation.

$$x + 3 = 5$$
$$x + \cancel{3} - \cancel{3} = 5 - 3$$
$$x = 2$$

When a problem has more than one
operation, follow these steps:
First get the term with the variable
by itself on one side of equation.
Then get the variable by itself.

$$\overset{\text{term}}{2y} - \overset{\text{term}}{1} = 9$$
$$2y - \cancel{1} + \cancel{1} = 9 + 1$$
$$2y = 10$$
$$\frac{2y}{2} = \frac{10}{2}$$
$$y = 5$$

Two-Step Equations

Solve 3x + 12 = 48. Check your solution.

Step 1: Write the equation.

$$3x + 12 = 48$$

Step 2: Get the term with the variable ($3x$)
by itself on one side of the equation.
Since 12 is added to ($3x$), subtract 12
from each side.

$$3x + 12 = 48$$
$$\underline{ - 12 \quad - 12}$$
$$3x = 36$$

Step 3: A multiplication problem is left.
Get the variable by itself using division.
Divide each side of the equation by 3.

$$\frac{\cancel{3}x}{\cancel{3}} = \frac{36}{3}$$
$$x = 12$$

Step 4: Check the solution. Remember,
ALWAYS use the order of operations when
there is more than one operation (see
pages 40–41). The solution is correct.

$$3x + 12 = 48$$
$$3(12) + 12 = 48$$
$$36 + 12 = 48$$
$$x = 12$$

Problems with Parentheses

Vito's family went to a water park. His sister won a free park pass. The total cost for his family's passes was $124.75. If each pass cost $24.95, how many people are in Vito's family? Write an algebraic equation and solve it to find the solution.

Step 1: This word equation shows how the total price is related to the number of passes bought.

total price equals price of one pass times number of passes bought

You want to find the number of people in Vito's family. The number of passes bought is the same as the number of people in Vito's family minus one for his sister. Replace the number of passes bought in the word equation with the number of people in Vito's family minus one.

total price equals price of one pass times (number of people in the family minus one)

Step 2: Replace words with numbers, symbols, and variables, using a variable for the value you don't know.

Let x = number of people in Vito's family

total price equals price of one pass times (number of people in the family minus one)

$$\$124.75 = \$24.95(x - 1)$$

Step 3: When the variable is inside parentheses, use inverse operations for the operations outside the parentheses first. The variable term $(x - 1)$ is multiplied by $24.95, so divide both sides of the equation by $24.95. $124.75 ÷ $24.95 = 5

$$\frac{\$124.75}{\$24.95} = \frac{\$24.95(x - 1)}{\$24.95}$$

$$5 = x - 1$$

Step 4: Inside the parentheses there is a subtraction problem. Get the variable by itself using addition. Add 1 to each side.

$$5 = x - 1$$
$$\underline{+1 \qquad +1}$$
$$6 = x$$

Step 5: Check the solution.
The solution is correct.

$$x = 6$$

There are 6 people in Vito's family.

$$\$124.75 = \$24.95(x - 1)$$
$$\$124.75 = \$24.95(6 - 1)$$
$$\$124.75 = \$24.95(5)$$
$$\$124.75 = 124.75$$

㉖ Inequalities

An inequality compares two expressions using an inequality sign.

Inequality Signs

The symbol > means "greater than."

The symbol ≥ means "greater than or equal to."

The symbol < means "less than."

The symbol ≤ means "less than or equal to."

Word Sentences

Write an inequality for the following sentence: The age of students in the senior gymnastics class is 12 or older.

Step 1: Chose a variable to represent the number or numbers you don't know (the age of the students).

Let a = age of students

A **solution set** includes all the numbers that make an inequality true.

For the inequality $a \geq 12$, the solution set is 12 and every number greater than 12.

Step 2: Decide which inequality sign is needed. The students are 12 or older. That means their age can be equal to 12 or greater than 12.

greater than or equal to: ≥

Step 3: Write the inequality.

$$a \geq 12$$

Number Lines

Graph the solution set for x ≤ 3 on a number line.

Step 1: Draw a number line that includes the number 3.

Step 2: Draw a solid circle on the number 3.
A solid circle shows that the number 3 is part of the answer.

Step 3: Since *x* is less than or equal to 3, the solution set includes 3 and all the numbers to the left of 3 on the number line. Draw a line with an arrow over the number line to show the rest of the solution set.

Graph the solution set for x > ⁻1 on a number line.

Step 1: Draw a number line that includes the number ⁻1.

Step 2: Draw an open circle on the number ⁻1. An open circle shows that the number ⁻1 is NOT part of the answer.

Step 3: Since *x* is greater than ⁻1, the solution set is all the numbers to the right of ⁻1 on the number line. Draw a line with an arrow over the number line to show the rest of the solution set.

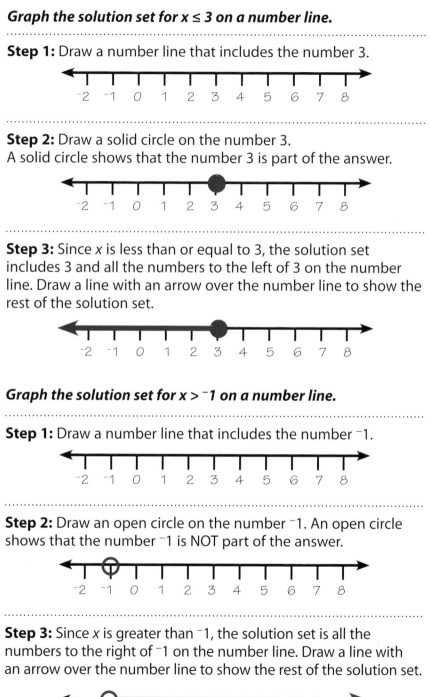

Inequalities are solved like equations. Get the variable by itself on one side of the inequality sign.

Addition Inequalities

Solve and graph the inequality $x + 5 > 3$.

Step 1: Write the inequality.

$$x + 5 > 3$$

Step 2: Use inverse operations to get the variable by itself on one side of the inequality sign. Use subtraction for numbers that are added. Subtract 5 from each side of the inequality.

$$x + 5 - 5 > 3 - 5$$

Step 3: Do the operations. Adding 5 and subtracting 5 cancel each other out. $3 - 5 = {}^-2$
$$x > {}^-2$$

$$x + \cancel{5} - \cancel{5} > 3 - 5$$
$$x > {}^-2$$

Step 4: Graph the inequality $x > {}^-2$ on a number line.

Step 5: Check your answer. You cannot check every number in the solution set, but you can check a few to test your solution set. Check any number from the solution set. Let's check the number 0. Put the number into the original inequality and see if the result is true.

$$x + 5 > 3$$
$$0 + 5 > 3$$
$$5 > 3$$

5 is greater than 3, so 0 is part of the solution set.

Now check a number that is NOT in the solution set. Let's check −2.
3 is NOT greater than 3, so −2 is NOT part of the solution set.

$$x + 5 > 3$$
$${}^-2 + 5 > 3$$
$$3 \not> 3$$

Subtraction Inequalities

Solve and graph the inequality $x - 16 \leq 20$.

Step 1: Write the inequality.

$$x - 16 \leq 20$$

Step 2: Use inverse operations to get the variable by itself on one side of the inequality sign. Use addition for numbers that are subtracted.
Add 16 to each side of the inequality.

$$\begin{aligned} x - 16 &\leq 20 \\ +16 \quad &\quad +16 \end{aligned}$$

Step 3: Do the operations.
Subtracting 16 and adding 16 cancel each other out. $20 + 16 = 36$

$$x \leq 36$$

$$\begin{aligned} x - 16 &\leq 20 \\ +16 \quad &\quad +16 \\ \hline x \quad\quad &\leq 36 \end{aligned}$$

Step 4: Graph the inequality $x \leq 36$ on a number line.

Step 5: Check a few numbers to test your solution set.
Check any number from the solution set.
Let's check the number 33.
Put the number into the original inequality and see if the result is true.

$$x - 16 \leq 20$$
$$33 - 16 \leq 20$$
$$17 \leq 20$$

17 is less than or equal to 20, so 33 is part of the solution set.

Now check a number that is NOT in the solution set. Let's check 40.

$$x - 16 \leq 20$$
$$40 - 16 \leq 20$$
$$24 \nleq 20$$

24 is NOT less than or equal to 20, so 40 is NOT part of the solution set.

> When you add or subtract the same value on each side of an inequality, the inequality stays true.
> $5 > 0$ True
> $5 + 5 > 0 + 5$
> $10 > 5$ Still true!

Solving Inequalities: Multiplication and Division

Solving multiplication and division inequalities is similar to, but not exactly the same as, solving equations.

Reversing the Sign

You can multiply or divide both sides of an inequality by a positive number, and it remains true.

2 < 10	True	**16 > 4**	True
2(10) < 10(10)		**16 ÷ 4 > 4 ÷ 4**	
20 < 100	Still true	**4 > 1**	Still true

When you multiply or divide both sides of an inequality by a negative number, the sign reverses.

2 < 10	True	**16 > 4**	True
2(⁻10) < 10(⁻10)		**16 ÷ ⁻4 > 4 ÷ ⁻4**	
⁻20 < ⁻100	NOT True	**⁻4 > ⁻1**	NOT True
−20 > −100	Reversed sign, True	**−4 < −1**	Reversed sign, True

Multiplication Inequalities

Solve 4n > 32.

Step 1: Write the inequality. $4n > 32$

Step 2: Get the variable, *n*, by itself. $\dfrac{4n}{4} > \dfrac{32}{4}$
Since the variable is multiplied by a
number, use division.
Divide each side of the inequality by the coefficient, 4.

Step 3: Do the operations.
$32 \div 4 = 8$

$$\frac{4n}{4} > \frac{32}{4}$$
$$n > 8$$

n > 8

Step 4: Test a solution.
Let's test 10, since $10 > 8$.

$$4n > 32$$
$$4(10) > 32$$
$$40 > 32$$

40 is greater than 32, so 10 is part of the solution set.

Division Inequalities

Solve $\frac{x}{-4} < 15$.

Step 1: Write the equation.

$$\frac{x}{-4} < 15$$

Step 2: Get the variable, x, by itself. Since the variable is being divided by $^-4$, multiply both sides of the equation by $^-4$. When you multiply by a negative number, reverse the direction of the inequality sign.

$$\frac{x}{-4}(^-4) > 15(^-4)$$

< *becomes* >

Step 3: Multiply. Dividing by $^-4$ and multiplying by $^-4$ cancel each other out. $15 \times ^-4 = ^-60$

$$\frac{x}{-4}(^-4) > 15(^-4)$$

$$\frac{x}{-4}(\frac{^-4}{1}) > 15(^-4)$$

$$x > ^-60$$

Step 4: Test a solution.
Let's test 4, since $4 > ^-60$, and 4 is easy to divide by $^-4$.
$^-1$ is less than 15, so 4 is part of the solution set.

$$\frac{x}{-4} < 15$$

$$\frac{4}{-4} < 15$$

$$^-1 < 15$$

x > $^-60$

Further Reading

Books

Bluman, Allan G. *Pre-Algebra Demystified*. New York: McGraw⊠Hill, 2011.

McKellar, Danica. *Hot X: Algebra Exposed*. New York: Hudson Street Press, 2010.

———. *Kiss My Math: Showing Pre-Algebra Who's Boss*. New York: Hudson Street Press, 2008.

Sterling, Mary Jane. *Algebra I Workbook For Dummies*. Indianapolis, Ind.: Wiley Publishers, Inc., 2011.

Zegarelli, Mark. *Pre-Algebra Essentials For Dummies*. Indianapolis, Ind.: Wiley Publishers, Inc., 2010.

Zev, Marc, Kevin B. Segal, and Nathan Levy. *101 Things Everyone Should Know About Math*. Washington, D.C.: Science Naturally!, 2010.

Internet Addresses

The Math Forum. "Ask Dr. Math" © 1994–2012.
<http://mathforum.org/library/drmath/sets/mid_algebra.html>

Banfill, J. AAA Math. "Algebra". © 2012.
<http://www.aaamath.com/alg.htm>

Index